NBA CHAMPIONSHIPS:

1955, 1967, 1983

ALL-TIME LEADING SCORER:

HAL GREER (1958–73):

21,586 POINTS

PHILA
SPALDING

THE NBA: A HISTORY OF HOOPS

PHILADELPHIA 76ERS

BY JIM WHITING

CREATIVE EDUCATION CREATIVE PAPERBACKS

Published by Creative Education
and Creative Paperbacks

P.O. Box 227, Mankato, Minnesota 56002

Creative Education and Creative Paperbacks
are imprints of The Creative Company

www.thecreativecompany.us

Design by Blue Design; production by Joe Kahnke

Printed in the United States of America

Photographs by Alamy (Steven M. Falk/Philadelphia Inquirer/TNS/Alamy Live News/Tribune Content Agency LLC, REUTERS/Tim Schaffer), AP Images (ASSOCIATED PRESS), Getty Images (Afro American Newspapers/Gado, Bettmann, Nathaniel S. Butler/NBAE, Jonathan Daniel/Stringer/Getty Images Sport, Stephen Dunn/Getty Images Sport, Focus on Sport, Jesse D. Garrabrant/NBAE, Barry Gossage/NBAE, Drew Hallowell, Walter Iooss Jr./NBAE, Mitchell Leff/Getty Images Sport, Neil Leifer/NBAE, Steve Lipofsky, Manny Millan/SI, NBA Photo Library/NBAE, Dick Raphael/NBAE, Dick Raphael/SI, Jon SooHoo/NBAE, John G. Zimmerman/Time & Life Pictures), iStockphoto (f11photo)

Library of Congress Cataloging-in-Publication Data

Names: Whiting, Jim, 1943- author.

Title: Philadelphia 76ers / Jim Whiting.

Series: The NBA: A History of Hoops.

Includes bibliographical references and index.

Summary: This high-interest title summarizes the history of the Philadelphia 76ers professional basketball team, highlighting memorable events and noteworthy players such as Julius Erving.

Identifiers: LCCN 2017006898 / ISBN 978-1-60818-857-4 (hardcover) / ISBN 978-1-62832-460-0 (pbk) / ISBN 978-1-56660-905-0 (eBook)

Subjects: LCSH: 1. Philadelphia 76ers (Basketball team)—History—Juvenile literature. 2. Philadelphia 76ers (Basketball team)—Biography—Juvenile literature.

Classification: LCC GV885.52.P45 W446 2017 / DDC 796.323/640974811—dc23

CCSS: RI.4.1, 2, 3, 4; RI.5.1, 2, 4; RI.6.1, 2, 3; RF.4.3, 4; RF.5.3, 4; RH. 6-8. 4, 5, 7

First Edition HC 9 8 7 6 5 4 3 2 1

First Edition PBK 9 8 7 6 5 4 3 2 1

76
25

CONTENTS

Called the "City of Brotherly Love," **PHILADELPHIA** served as the nation's capital while Washington, D.C., was being built.

THE LITTLE CITY THAT COULD

As he did thousands of times during his spectacular career in the National Basketball Association (NBA), Julius "Dr. J" Erving drove toward the hoop. His Philadelphia 76ers were playing

"HERE I WAS, TRYING TO WIN A CHAMPIONSHIP, AND MY MOUTH JUST DROPPED OPEN.... IT'S STILL THE GREATEST MOVE I'VE EVER SEEN IN A BASKETBALL GAME."

the Los Angeles Lakers. It was the 1980 NBA Finals. He passed the man guarding him and soared toward the right side of the basket. Lakers center Kareem Abdul-Jabbar loomed in his path. Erving twisted his body away from Abdul-Jabbar. He was now behind the backboard. It seemed likely that he would come down still holding the ball. That would result in a traveling violation.

Somehow Erving defied gravity. He hung in the air. He shifted his body slightly to the left. He reached under the backboard and scooped up a shot from the far side of the basket. It went in! The Lakers were stunned. "Here I was, trying to win a championship, and my mouth just dropped open," said Lakers guard Magic Johnson. "I thought, 'What should we do? Should we take the ball out, or should we ask him to do it again?' It's still the greatest move I've ever seen in a basketball game." The "Baseline Move" helped the 76ers win 105–102.

The 76ers' story began in 1946. Syracuse, New York, bowling alley owner Danny Biasone established the Syracuse Nationals in the National Basketball League (NBL). The team had losing records its first two years. Sharpshooting rookie Dolph Schayes helped the team to a 40–23 mark in 1948–49. The following season, the NBL merged with the Basketball Association of America (BAA). The new league was the NBA. The Nationals had the league's best record (51–13) in its first year. They lost

Legendary highflier **JULIUS ERVING** earned All-Star honors in each of his 16 years of professional hoops.

LEGENDS OF THE HARDWOOD

THE MAN WHO SAVED PRO BASKETBALL

Many games in the late 1940s and early 1950s were low-scoring and boring. As *Sports Illustrated* writer Leigh Montville explains, "The strategy of the day had become inaction. Get a lead. Hold the ball.... Teams were deciding to stall earlier and earlier in the game." Attendance declined. Syracuse owner Danny Biasone knew the game needed more action. He wanted to force teams to take more shots. So he invented the shot clock. Teams had to shoot within 24 seconds or give up the ball. The shot clock was first used in the 1954–55 season. Scores increased by more than 14 points a game. "Danny Biasone saved the NBA with the 24-second rule," said coach Charlie Eckman.

in the Finals to the Minneapolis Lakers. The team played well following that season. But it couldn't get past the Eastern Division finals. The Nationals finally broke through in 1955. They defeated the Fort Wayne Pistons four games to three. Eighth-round draft pick George King was the unlikely hero. He sank a free throw in the closing seconds of Game 7. That gave the Nationals a 92–91 lead. Then he stole the inbounds pass to preserve the edge. The Nationals were NBA champions! The team continued to play well. It always made the playoffs.

Syracuse was the smallest city in the NBA. So the Nationals and their fans felt they were not treated with as much respect. "The people would come out, and the fact that 'Little Syracuse is playing Boston, Syracuse is playing New York?' The fans would go nuts when we beat them. And we won most of the time," said Schayes. "We were David

LEGENDS OF THE HARDWOOD

THE JACKIE ROBINSON OF THE NBA

EARL LLOYD, FORWARD, 6-FOOT-5, 1952–58

Everyone knows Jackie Robinson, the first black player in Major League Baseball. Hardly anyone knows Earl Lloyd, the first black man to play in an NBA game. The historic date was October 31, 1950. Lloyd scored six points for the Washington Capitols as they played the Rochester Royals. Lloyd was drafted into the U.S. Army. He returned in 1952 and began playing for the Nationals. Fellow players hardly ever made racist comments. But fans were not as kind. "They yell stuff like, 'Go back to Africa,'" he said. "You would often hear the N-word." Lloyd used those comments as motivation. He was inducted into the Naismith Memorial Basketball Hall of Fame in 2003.

Sharpshooter and rebounder **DOLPH SCHAYES** logged 14 seasons with the team before becoming coach.

vs. Goliath." Unfortunately, "David" had several problems. The Nationals played in the NBA's smallest arena. Fan support was falling. Player salaries were rising. Biasone was losing money. In 1963, he reluctantly sold the team. A group of Philadelphia businessmen bought the Nationals. They moved the team to their hometown.

PHILA
13
CELTICS

Towering center **WILT CHAMBERLAIN** was named league MVP three times as a Sixer.

THE BEST EVER?

The 76ers weren't the first pro hoops team in Philadelphia. The Philadelphia Warriors began playing in the BAA in 1946. They became part of the NBA three years later. They won the title in 1956. Three years later, the Warriors signed massive Philadelphia native Wilt Chamberlain. He was a 7-foot-1 center who became one of the league's top scorers. In 1962, he scored 100 points in a game. A few months later, California businessman Franklin Mieuli purchased the team. He moved it to San Francisco. Philadelphia basketball fans didn't have anyone to cheer for.

That didn't last long. The Nationals arrived in Philadelphia the following season. The owners wanted a new name. Several people suggested 76ers. That honored the signing of the Declaration of Independence in Philadelphia on July 4, 1776. The name is often shortened to Sixers. The new team wasn't an instant hit. Fewer than 6,000 fans turned out when the 76ers played the Warriors. The Sixers pulled out a 106–102 overtime win. They won just 33 other games. Chamberlain returned to Philadelphia during the 1964–65 season. He helped the Sixers advance to the Eastern Division finals in 1965 and 1966. But Boston defeated Philadelphia both times.

It was a different story in the 1966–67 season. Many people believe that 76ers team was the NBA's greatest ever. Every position had a solid starter, such as forward Billy "The Kangaroo Kid" Cunningham and point guard Hal Greer. The bench was also deep and talented. The Sixers won an NBA-record 68 games. They went on to win the NBA title by

Quietly consistent **HAL GREER** averaged 19.2 points per game over his 15-year career.

"IT WAS A BEAUTIFUL, BEAUTIFUL SEASON," GREER SAID. "WE HAD EVERYTHING. WE KNEW WE WERE GOING TO WIN MOST OF OUR GAMES—IT WAS JUST A MATTER OF BY HOW MUCH."

The Sixers bounded through the playoffs and conquered the Warriors for the 1967 NBA title.

defeating the Warriors. "It was a beautiful, beautiful season," Greer said. "We had everything. We knew we were going to win most of our games—it was just a matter of by how much." With almost the same lineup the following year, another title seemed likely. The Sixers met Boston in the division finals again. They won three of the first four games. But the Celtics battled back to win the series.

LEGENDS OF THE HARDWOOD

MR. CONSISTENCY

HAL GREER, POINT GUARD, 6-FOOT-2, 1958–73

Hal Greer was a small, skinny guard when the Nationals drafted him. He didn't unpack his bags at training camp. He didn't think he had much of a chance to make the team. He was wrong. Greer became a 10-time NBA All-Star. Yet he never called attention to himself. "If there were an award given for a player who is most respected by basketball insiders while getting the minimum public appreciation, Greer could win hands down," wrote a sportswriter. Greer played hard every game, every year. "Consistency," he said. "For me, that was the thing. I would like to be remembered as a great, consistent player." He remains the team's all-time leading scorer.

CELTICS
16
PHILA
32

BILLY CUNNINGHAM was known as "The Kangaroo Kid" for his remarkable leaping ability.

The Sixers traded Chamberlain soon afterward. While they remained a good team, they were no longer a serious championship contender. They lost in the first round of the playoffs in the next three seasons. Philly plummeted to a 30–52 record in 1971–72. It was the first time the team didn't make the playoffs. Still, no one expected what happened the following season. The Sixers lost their first 15 games. Later that season, they had a 20-game losing streak. They finished with just nine wins. It was the worst performance of any team in NBA history. Local media mocked the team as the "9-and-73ers." They improved to win 25 and 34 games in the next 2 seasons.

Although opponents tried their best to block him, **DR. J** was an unstoppable force.

THE DOCTOR MAKES A HOUSE CALL IN PHILLY

The Sixers returned to the playoffs in 1976. But they lost in the first round to the Buffalo Braves. Help was on the way. Erving joined the Sixers the following season. Philadelphia surged to the NBA

Unselfish guard **MAURICE CHEEKS** often stole the ball from opponents and shared it with teammates.

Finals again. It lost to the Portland Trail Blazers in six games. Philly made the Finals again in 1980 and 1982. Both times they lost to the Lakers. Team officials believed they needed a dominating center to win the championship. So they signed 6-foot-10 Moses Malone. He was a two-time Most Valuable Player (MVP). Philadelphia had the league's best record with 65 wins. Malone won his third MVP award. Before the playoffs, he made his famous "fo-fo-fo" prediction. He meant the 76ers would sweep all their series by winning four games each time. He was almost correct. The team swept the New York Knicks and lost a game to the Milwaukee Bucks in the Eastern Conference finals. Then it buried the

LEGENDS OF THE HARDWOOD

THE DOCTOR IS IN THE HOUSE

JULIUS ERVING, SMALL FORWARD/GUARD, 6-FOOT-7, 1976–87

Julius Erving nearly didn't become a 76er. He played for the New York Nets. The Nets joined the NBA in 1976. They had to pay a $3-million entry fee. They also had to pay $4.8 million to the New York Knicks for "invading" their territory. The Nets offered Dr. J to the Knicks instead of paying all that money. The Knicks said no. The Sixers offered the Nets $3 million for Erving's contract. The desperate Nets agreed to the deal. Erving immediately made the Sixers a serious contender. "Julius was the first player I ever remember who transcended sports and was known by one name—Doctor," said coach Billy Cunningham.

One of the game's best-ever centers, **MOSES MALONE** led the league in rebounds per game for three Sixers seasons.

Lakers in four games to capture the title. "The difference from last year was Moses," said coach Billy Cunningham.

Almost the same lineup returned the following year. Fans hoped for a repeat performance. But Philadelphia lost in the first round of the playoffs to the New York Nets. The Sixers drafted power forward Charles Barkley before the 1984–85 season. He stood just 6-foot-6 but used all of his 250 pounds to snag many rebounds. The Sixers met the Celtics in the conference finals. They lost, four games to one. Two more early playoff exits followed. Then Erving retired. The Sixers sagged to 36 wins without him. They returned to the playoffs in the next three seasons but couldn't advance past the second round. During this time, Barkley was among the league leaders in scoring and rebounding. He became tired with what he saw as the team's lack

"SIR CHARLES" BARKLEY earned fame for his dominant play as well as his outrageous behavior.

of progress. Philly won only 35 games in the 1991–92 season. Barkley demanded to be traded.

Without Barkley, the Sixers kept getting worse. They won just 26, 25, and 24 games in the next 3 seasons. They fell to just 18 wins in 1995–96. That was the second-worst in team history. But there was a silver lining. The team got the top choice in the 1996 NBA Draft. Philadelphia chose point guard Allen Iverson. He had been an All-American at Georgetown University. "He's a special athlete and a special competitor, and he has leadership ability," general manager Brad Greenberg said. "He made it an easy decision." Standing just 6 feet, Iverson was the shortest first pick in NBA history.

LEGENDS OF THE HARDWOOD

DRAFT DAY DISASTER

The Sixers seemed ready to contend for the NBA title again in 1986–87. They had veteran stars Moses Malone and Julius Erving. Charles Barkley would soon become a star. The Sixers also had the first pick in the 1986 Draft. They traded that pick to Cleveland for guard Roy Hinson (pictured). The Cavaliers used the pick on center Brad Daugherty. Then the Sixers swapped Malone for Washington Bullets center Jeff Ruland. Hinson never lived up to expectations. Ruland was plagued with knee problems. On the other hand, Daugherty became Cleveland's leading scorer. Malone averaged double-doubles for the next four years. Some people say the Sixers never fully recovered from those trades.

Dynamic point guard **ALLEN IVERSON** made up for his small stature with confidence and superb skills.

IVERSON TAKES OVER

Iverson's size didn't seem to bother him. "I try to put pressure on the defense," he explained. "I am always, always looking to score, always looking to make something happen on the court." And that was exactly what he did. "The Answer," as he was nicknamed, averaged more than 23 points, 7 assists, 4 rebounds, and 2 steals a game. He was selected Rookie of the Year. Unfortunately, he couldn't answer all the team's questions by himself. Philadelphia improved to only 22 wins in his first season and 31 in his second.

By then the team had hired veteran coach Larry Brown. Brown overhauled the roster. Under his guidance, the Sixers went 28–22 in the strike-shortened 1998–99 season. That record returned them to the playoffs for the first time in eight years. But they lost to the Indiana Pacers in the second round. Almost exactly the same thing happened the following season. The team surged to 49 wins. Again they lost to the Pacers in the second round.

Fans wanted more. They got it in the 2000–01 season. The Sixers had

LEGENDS OF THE HARDWOOD

LITTLE MAN, BIG HEART

ALLEN IVERSON, POINT GUARD, 6 FEET, 1996–2006, 2009–10

Allen Iverson was officially six feet tall. Many people think he was shorter. He never let his size get in his way. He led both his high school basketball and football teams to state titles. In college and the pros, he drove the lane fearlessly. He was often knocked down. He got right back up. As a 76er, Iverson led the league in scoring four times. “He had an unbelievable career,” said coach Larry Brown. “I don’t think any little player in the history of our game impacted the game like him.” Fellow superstar LeBron James added, “He played like a 6-foot-8 2-guard [shooting guard].... You could never question his heart. Ever. He gave it his all.”

IVERSON outmaneuvered veteran players and attacked the rim against much larger opponents.

the best record in the Eastern Conference. They swept the major awards. Iverson led the league in scoring with more than 31 points a game. He was named MVP. Midseason acquisition and center Dikembe Mutombo was Defensive Player of the Year. Guard Aaron McKie was Sixth Man of the Year. Brown was Coach of the Year. After an easy series win over Indiana, the Sixers barely defeated the Toronto Raptors in the second round. They won Game 7 by a single point. Milwaukee pushed them to seven games as well. Now they faced the heavily favored Lakers in the Finals. Iverson scored 48 points as the Sixers won Game 1. But the Lakers swept the next four games.

Backup center **AARON McKIE** notched two triple-double games during the 2000–01 season.

First-round draft pick **ANDRE IGUODALA** helped his team reach the playoffs as a rookie.

The Sixers were eliminated in early rounds of the playoffs the following two seasons. Brown unexpectedly resigned near the end of the 2002–03 season. Iverson was injured for much of the following season. He also clashed with the new coaching staff. The 76ers missed the playoffs for the first time in six years. The addition of All-Star power forward Chris Webber and rookie small forward Andre Iguodala helped the team rebound the following season. Iguodala was named to the All-Rookie first team. But the Sixers lost in the first round of the playoffs. They missed the playoffs again in 2005–06. Iverson was traded shortly after the start of the following season.

IGUODALA earned All-Star status in 2011–12 but was traded after the season.

Versatile swingman **EVAN TURNER** could play a variety of roles on the court.

BOTTOMING OUT ... AND BACK UP?

The 76ers squeaked into the playoffs three of the next four years. But they lost in the first round every time. In 2011–12, the team's Jrue Holiday became one of the league's best point guards. Iguodala

Point guard **JRUE HOLIDAY** worked hard to improve his game and team leadership.

was named to the All-Star Game. The Sixers finally won a first-round series. They became just the sixth number-eight seed to topple a number-one seed when they beat the Chicago Bulls. It was their first playoff win in nine years. The 76ers pushed Boston to seven games in the next round before losing. Philadelphia traded Iguodala after the season. Part of what it received in return was All-Star center Andrew Bynum. But Bynum got hurt and didn't play a single game. Philadelphia was last in the league in scoring. It won only 34 games.

The 76ers decided to go into full rebuilding mode. They traded Holiday and released Bynum. Other players were also released or chose to leave. The Sixers drafted Michael Carter-Williams to replace Holiday. He led all rookies in points, assists, steals, and rebounds. He was named Rookie of the Year. The Sixers began the 2013–14 season with three wins. But they won only 16 more games. When they reached 26 losses in a row, that tied the all-time NBA record.

The following season, the Sixers lost their first 17 games. They traded Carter-Williams and finished 18–64. Philadelphia began the 2015–16 season by dropping their first 18 games. That tied the NBA record for losses at the beginning of the season. They had lost the last 10 games of the previous season. That string of 28 consecutive losses set an NBA record. It was also the longest losing streak in any professional sport. The Sixers finished with a record of 10–72. It was the second-worst mark in team history. Despite the losses, young players such as center Jahlil Okafor gained valuable experience. That experience paid off as the 76ers rebounded to win 26 games. Center Joel Embiid missed his first two seasons because of injury. He played in just 31 games in 2016–17 but averaged 20 points and 8 rebounds. Rookie forward Ben Simmons missed the entire season. When healthy, they were projected to be the cornerstones of the franchise going forward.

People ridiculed the 76ers for being so bad in recent years. But the team still has one of the league's best historical records. Nine times it advanced to the Finals. Only the Celtics and Lakers have done that more often. Now the Sixers have one of the league's youngest rosters. As these players improve, fans look forward to many more playoff appearances.

Named to the 2014–15 All-Rookie first team, **NERLENS NOEL** was plagued with knee problems.

SELECTED BIBLIOGRAPHY

Ballard, Chris. *The Art of a Beautiful Game: The Thinking Fan's Tour of the NBA*. New York: Simon & Schuster, 2010.

Hareas, John. *Ultimate Basketball: More Than 100 Years of the Sport's Evolution*. New York: DK, 2004.

Hubbard, Jan, ed. *The Official NBA Basketball Encyclopedia*. 3rd edition. New York: Doubleday, 2000.

NBA.com. "Philadelphia 76ers." http://www.nba.com/sixers/.

Simmons, Bill. *The Book of Basketball: The NBA According to the Sports Guy*. New York: Ballantine, 2009.

Sports Illustrated. *Sports Illustrated Basketball's Greatest*. New York: Sports Illustrated, 2014.

WEBSITES

JR. NBA
http://jr.nba.com/

This kids site has games, videos, game results, team and player information, statistics, and more.

JULIUS ERVING—BASELINE MOVE
https://www.youtube.com/watch?v=B93gof7E1BM

This video depicts Julius Erving's famous shot against the Lakers. Immediately following is Dr. J's Top 10 Dunks and other notable shots.

Note: Every effort has been made to ensure that any websites listed above were active at the time of publication. However, because of the nature of the Internet, it is impossible to guarantee that these sites will remain active indefinitely or that their contents will not be altered.

INDEX